This
book
belongs
to

ALEX

The New KIDS Book of

Book of

Bible People

The New Kids Book of Bible People

Copyright © 1999 Educational Publishing Concepts, Inc., Wheaton, IL

Published by New Kids Media™ in association with Baker Book House Company, Grand Rapids, Michigan.

ISBN 0-8010-4434-0

Printed in the United States of America

1 2 3 4 — 02 01 00 99

The New KIDS Book of
Book of

Bible People

Anne Adams

Illustrated by Marlene McAuley

Published in
association with

For my children
Michal and Alexandra Tyra

Dear Parents,

It's never too early to begin teaching the truths of the Bible to your children. The Junior Reference Series will help young children understand the meaning of major Bible passages and see God's daily involvement in the lives of his people. They will enjoy learning about Bible animals and how their personalities were used to explain how people sometimes behave. Our prayer is that this series will instill in your child a lifelong thirst for knowledge of the Bible and it's message of love.

The Publishers

Adam & Eve

God used dust to make Adam, the first man. Adam lived in the Garden of Eden. One of his jobs was to name the animals. God didn't want Adam to be alone, so he used one of Adam's ribs to make Eve, the first woman. She was Adam's wife. Together, they ruled over all of God's creatures.

God said Adam and Eve could eat the fruit of any tree except the Tree of Knowledge. But the devil tempted Eve to disobey God. She and Adam ate the forbidden fruit and sin came into the world. As punishment, they had to leave the garden. Later, they had many children including Cain and Abel.

CaiN & AbEL

Cain was the son of Adam and Eve and the first child born into the world. He grew up to be a farmer. His younger brother Abel was a shepherd. Adam and Eve taught both boys to serve God. Abel was a good man who hated sin, but Cain was rebellious and selfish.

One day both men gave offerings to God. Abel brought the finest of his flock which pleased God, but Cain's offering of vegetables did not. Cain was so jealous of his brother, he killed him. Abel was the first man on earth to die. God protected Cain from his enemies, but he had to leave home and wander around.

Noah

Long after God made the earth there was only one man who still loved God. His name was Noah. When Noah was 480 years old, God told him that he would send a flood on the whole earth. God told Noah to build an ark to save him and his family. Noah and his sons worked on the ark for 120 years. Noah warned people about the flood and begged them to repent.

When the ark was finished, Noah's family and two of every animal went inside. God shut the door and it rained until water flooded the earth. When the flood was over, Noah and his family left the ark. Noah lived to be 950 years old.

Abraham & Sarah

Abraham was first known as Abram.
God told him to go to the land of
Canaan. Abram trusted God so he went
to the new country with his wife Sarai
and his nephew Lot. God promised to
bless Abram. He said that his children
would have many children.

Sarai doubted she would have a
baby so she gave Abram her servant
Hagar to be his second wife. Hagar
gave birth to Ishmael, Abram's first
son. God changed Abram's name to
Abraham which means "father of many
nations," and Sarai became Sarah.
When Abraham was 100 years old,
Sarah gave birth to Isaac, the son
which God had promised them.

Isaac and Rebekah

Isaac was the only son of Abraham and Sarah. When he was a child, God tested Abraham's faith by telling him to sacrifice Isaac. Abraham loved his son but he trusted God and wanted to obey him. Abraham placed Isaac on an altar of wood and was ready to kill him when God stopped him.

Isaac was quiet and gentle, peaceful and patient, and anxious to do God's will. When he was forty years old, his father sent a servant to find a wife for Isaac. He returned with Rebekah and not long after, they were married. Isaac and Rebekah had twin sons, Esau and Jacob.

Esau and Jacob

Esau and Jacob were the twin sons of Isaac and Rebekah. Before they were born, God told Rebekah that her younger son would rule over her older son. When Esau grew up he didn't care about God or his birthright, a special blessing given to the oldest son by the father.

Esau sold his birthright to Jacob for a bowl of soup. When Isaac was old and blind, he was going to give Esau the blessing. Jacob tricked Isaac and stole the birthright.

Jacob married two sisters, Leah and Rachel. God called him Israel, and all of his children were called Israelites.

MOSES

When Moses was born to Hebrew slaves in Egypt, Pharaoh had ordered that all Hebrew baby boys be killed. Moses' mother hid him in a basket on the Nile River. His sister Miriam watched as Pharaoh's daughter found him and adopted him.

Moses became an Egyptian prince but he knew he was really a Hebrew. God called him to lead the Hebrews out of slavery in Egypt. God gave Moses the Ten Commandments to give to the people. Sadly, Moses' own sins kept him from entering the land God promised to the Israelites.

Aaron

Aaron was the brother of Moses and Miriam. God called him to help Moses lead the Hebrews from Egypt. He was a good speaker, so he did the talking when they went to Pharaoh. He used his rod to perform many miracles. When God told him to throw it to the ground, it changed into a snake.

After the Hebrews left Egypt, Aaron committed a great sin. While Moses was on the mountain receiving the Ten Commandments, Aaron helped the people make a golden calf to worship. God forgave Aaron when Moses begged him to. Aaron died before reaching the Promised Land.

Lot

L ot was Abraham's nephew. He went to Canaan with Abraham and settled near Sodom and Gomorrah. The people there were very bad, and God decided to destroy them. When he told Abraham about his plans Abraham asked God to save Lot. God agreed.

Lot saw two angels come to Sodom. He invited them to his home. He gave them food and asked them to spend the night. He also protected them from his evil neighbors. The angels led Lot's family out of the city and told them not to look back. But Lot's wife looked at the burning cities and she turned into a pillar of salt. Lot and his two daughters escaped.

Hagar and Ishmael

Hagar was Sarah's servant. When Sarah began to doubt that she would ever have a child, she gave Hagar to be Abraham's second wife. Hagar became pregnant and Sarah was mean to her. She tried to run away but an angel told her to go back. Hagar returned and gave birth to Abraham's son, Ishmael.

After Isaac was born, Ishmael often teased him. Sarah wanted Hagar and Ishmael gone, so Abraham sent them into the desert. God sent an angel to tell Hagar that God would make her son into a great nation. Ishmael became a fine hunter and archer and the forefather of the Arab people.

JOSEPH

Joseph was Jacob's favorite son. He even gave him a beautiful colored robe. His brothers were jealous of Joseph, and they decided to get rid of him. They sold him to men headed for Egypt and told their father that he was dead. Joseph was a slave in Pharaoh's house but God was with him, and he became an important ruler in Egypt.

During a great famine, Jacob's sons went to Egypt to buy corn from Joseph. They didn't recognize him, but Joseph knew them. He saw that they had changed, so he told them who he was. He invited them and his father to live in Egypt. Jacob rejoiced when he saw that his favorite son was alive!

JoShUa

Joshua was Moses' helper on the trip from Egypt to the Promised Land. He was also Israel's military leader. God allowed Joshua to come part way up the mountain when he gave Moses the Ten Commandments, and he was one of twelve men sent by Moses to check out the Promised Land. Of the twelve, only Joshua and Caleb believed that God would give them the land.

When Moses died, Joshua led the Israelites across the Jordan River into the Promised Land. He led them in the famous battle of Jericho before taking the rest of Canaan. Joshua was so loved that when he died at the age of 110, the country cried.

Deborah

Deborah was the only female judge in Israel's history. During her time judges ruled instead of kings. She sat in a tent beneath a palm tree called the "palm of Deborah." One of the problems she faced was that Jabin, the king of Canaan, was always threatening to attack Israel.

God told Deborah to tell General Barak to gather thousands of men and lead them to Mount Tabor where the army of Jabin was waiting.

When Deborah gave the signal, the Israelite army rushed down and defeated Jabin's men. Deborah and Barak were so happy, they sang a song of victory!

Gideon

Gideon was a great judge in Israel. During his rule, people called Midianites stole the cattle and ruined the crops of the Israelites. They made God's people very unhappy. God told Gideon to form an army to attack the Midianites. When thousands of men appeared, God told Gideon only 300 were needed.

The soldiers crept into the Midianites camp during the night. Each of the men had a trumpet and a jar with a torch inside. All at once, they blew their trumpets and broke their jars. The Midianites were so afraid and confused, they attacked one another and were defeated.

Samson

Samson was a judge in Israel. He was very strong, but he wasn't wise. Before he was born, an angel told his mother that her son would be a Nazirite, one who didn't cut his hair. The angel said Samson would help deliver the Israelites from the Philistines.

When Samson fell in love with Delilah, a Philistine, he told her that the secret of his strength was his hair. She told his secret, and the Philistines cut Samson's hair. His strength was gone and the Philistines captured him. When his hair grew back and his strength returned, Samson got revenge. He pulled down a whole temple killing many Philistines, but also himself.

Naomi and Ruth

When Naomi and her family lived in Israel, there was a famine and there was no more food to eat. They moved to Moab where Naomi's son married a woman named Ruth. Then Naomi's husband and sons all died. The women were left alone.

Naomi was sad and she wanted to return to Bethlehem. Ruth went with Naomi and took care of her by working in the fields to gather grain for food. Ruth worked for Boaz, a kind man who was a relative of Naomi. Soon, they fell in love and were married. Naomi helped take care of their son, Obed, who became the grandfather of the great King David.

Samuel

Samuel was a priest, a prophet, and Israel's last judge. Before his birth, his mother Hannah prayed that if God gave her a son, she would give him to serve God. When Samuel was born, Hannah kept her word. She brought him to the tabernacle where Eli the priest taught him to serve God.

As Israel's leader, Samuel told the Israelites to stop worshiping false gods. The Philistines found out where the Israelites were and planned an attack. Samuel prayed for God to rescue them. Suddenly, thunder boomed and the Philistines ran away. Later, Samuel anointed Saul and David as the first and second kings of Israel.

David

David was the greatest king of Israel. He had many talents, and did nearly everything well. As a young shepherd, he fought lions and bears to protect his flock. He played music to calm his sheep and was so good, King Saul asked him to be his musician.

David was still a young man when he volunteered to fight the giant Goliath. The Israelite soldiers were all afraid. David killed him with a sling and a stone, and became a hero to the people. That made King Saul jealous. For years Saul tried to kill David. David hid in the hills until Saul was killed in a battle. Samuel anointed David as the new king of Israel.

Saul

Saul was the first king of Israel but some people didn't think he should be king. One day when he was sent to look for his father's donkeys which had run away, he met Samuel. Samuel was impressed with the young man and secretly anointed him to be king. At that moment God changed Saul, and he became a child of God.

Saul sometimes did things his own way instead of listening to God. Once he was supposed to wait for Samuel to offer a sacrifice but Saul decided to do it himself. Samuel told him that because of his disobedience, God would remove him as king. Not long after, Saul was killed.

SOLOMON

Solomon was the third king of Israel and one of the most famous. He was the son of King David and the first king born to a king. In a dream, God told Solomon to ask for whatever he wanted. When Solomon asked for wisdom to rule his kingdom, God was happy. He gave Solomon wisdom as well as riches.

God let Solomon build the temple. He also built palaces and stables for his large collection of horses. After a while, Solomon began to care more about his possessions than he cared about God. He had seven hundred wives and even began to worship false idols. When Solomon died, Israel was falling apart.

ELIJAH

Elijah was a prophet who warned Israel's kings and people to turn from their evil ways. God taught Elijah that when he obeyed the Lord, he was kept safe and his needs were met. Once, during a famine, God sent Elijah to a ravine where ravens brought him meat every day.

When Elijah's ministry was nearly finished, God sent Elisha to him. While together, they were suddenly separated by a chariot and horses of fire. Elijah did not die, but instead was taken to heaven in a whirlwind. His cloak fell to Elisha which meant that he carried on the work of the great prophet.

ELISHA

Elisha was plowing his field when the prophet Elijah came and threw his cloak over his shoulders. Elisha was chosen to take the place of Elijah. As the time came for Elijah to go to God, Elisha would not leave him. When Elijah was carried to heaven in a whirlwind, Elisha received his cloak and a double share of his spirit.

Elisha became a prophet and God used him to do many miracles. He cured the bitter waters of Jericho with salt, made an iron axhead float, and he restored lives. Even after Elisha died, he was still performing miracles. When a dead man's body touched Elisha's bones, the man came alive!

JOASH

Joash was a baby when his father, King Ahaziah of Judah, was killed. The king's mother tried to murder everyone in the family so she could be queen. Joash's aunt and uncle hid him away. He was only seven-years-old when he became the king of Judah.

While Joash was still a child, his uncle Jehoiada helped him rule the country. Joash was a godly king. He even fixed the broken temple. After Jehoiada died, Joash turned away from God. He killed his uncle's son, then was put to death by his own servants. He ruled for forty years, but his sin kept him from being buried in the tombs of the kings.

JONAH

Jonah was a prophet and a missionary, but he didn't always obey God. The Lord sent him to Nineveh to preach to the evil people, but he didn't go. Jonah was afraid the people would listen, repent, and be forgiven. He thought they should die for their sins. Jonah got on a ship and sailed away from Nineveh.

When a storm came, the sailors thought Jonah was the cause. They tossed him overboard, and he was swallowed by a huge fish. Jonah sat in the fish's belly and prayed. After three days, he was spit out on the shore. When God called Jonah to Nineveh again, he went. Jonah learned that God's love and mercy is for all people.

DANIEL

Daniel was a young man in Judah when his country was attacked by Babylon. Daniel was captured and served in the king's court where God used him as a prophet. He told the king the meaning of his dreams. The king was so impressed that he made Daniel chief of all his wise men.

When Daniel became one of the three top rulers of the country, the other rulers were jealous. They wanted to get rid of him. They knew Daniel loved God, so they told the king to make it unlawful to pray. Daniel prayed anyway, and he was thrown into a den of lions. God was with him and he wasn't hurt at all!

ESTHER

Esther was a Jewish orphan but she grew up to be the queen who saved her people. She was raised by her cousin Mordecai who wouldn't let her tell anyone she was Jewish. King Xerxes married her, but he didn't know she was a Jew.

Haman was advisor to the king, and he hated the Jews because they wouldn't bow down to him. He told Xerxes that the Jews should be killed. The king agreed, not knowing about his wife. Esther risked her life by telling the king she was Jewish. In the end, Xerxes spared the Jews. But it was really Esther's courage which saved her people.

Job

Job was a wealthy man with a wife and ten children. He owned lots of land and livestock. But above all, Job loved God. Satan said Job loved God because of all he had. He wanted to take away Job's blessings. God agreed, because he knew Job didn't love him because of his blessings.

His children were killed and he lost his livestock. But Job didn't blame God. Satan was angry, and he wanted to make Job sick. God agreed, because he knew Job wasn't godly because he was healthy. Job got sick, but he still loved God. God restored his health and blessed him with more children and more wealth than before.

Ezekiel

Ezekiel was in Jerusalem, training to be a priest, when his country was captured by Babylon. Ezekiel helped the captive Jews learn how to worship without a temple. During this time, God called him to be a prophet and gave him dreams and visions. Some of these told of the future. Some taught the Jews to be obedient.

God told Ezekiel that Jerusalem would be destroyed. Ezekiel was to make a model of the city and place soldiers around it. Then God told him to lay next to it. Ezekiel did this every day for over a year. This helped the people to understand and remember what God was telling them.

Joseph and Mary

Joseph and Mary lived in Nazareth and were engaged to be married. The angel Gabriel told Mary she would give birth to the Son of God. She was to name the baby "Jesus." Mary loved God and she was honored to be chosen to be the mother of the Messiah.

The angel also appeared to Joseph and explained that Mary would be the mother of Jesus and the Holy Spirit was the father. Joseph married Mary as planned. When Jesus was born, Joseph was his earthly father. He cared for Jesus and taught him to be a carpenter like him. Joseph and Mary also had other children. They were Jesus' brothers and sisters.

JeSUS

Jesus is God's son. He was the Savior of the world, so God sent him to be born on earth. He was raised by his mother Mary and her husband, Joseph. By the time he was twelve, everyone knew he had great wisdom.

Jesus was thirty when God called him to travel and teach. He called twelve disciples and taught them about God. Together, they walked from place to place. Huge crowds gathered to hear Jesus teach about God's love. Jesus knew he had to die on earth in order to bring salvation to the world. After he was crucified, he rose again and went to heaven. He sits beside God and speaks to him for us.

JOHN THE BAPTIST

John the Baptist was the prophet of God who prepared the way for Jesus. He was born just six months before Jesus. He wore clothes made of camel's hair, and he ate locusts and wild honey. Crowds came from all over to hear John preach about the coming of Jesus. He warned people to repent of their sins. Then, he baptized them in the Jordan River.

Jesus went to John to be baptized. At first, John refused, he didn't think he was worthy to baptize the Savior. It wasn't long after baptizing Jesus that John's ministry ended. When he was killed, Jesus called his friend a "burning and a shining light."

Peter

Peter was one of the first disciples chosen by Jesus. He was originally named Simon. When he and his brother Andrew were fishing on the Sea of Galilee, Jesus called them to follow him. The brothers dropped their nets and went. Jesus changed Simon's name to Peter which meant, "the rock."

Peter loved Jesus and was the first disciple to know he was the Messiah. But, Peter wasn't perfect. Three times he denied knowing Jesus. Later, he cried for what he had done. After Jesus went to heaven, Peter preached about the kingdom of God. He was thrown in prison several times for his faith and later killed.

ANdreW

Andrew was a fisherman, the brother of Peter, and one of the first disciples called by Jesus. He was first a disciple of John the Baptist. One day, when he and John saw Jesus, John called Jesus the "Lamb of God." Andrew left right away, followed Jesus, and spent the day with him. He found his brother Peter, and he led him to Jesus.

One time the disciples were with Jesus when a crowd of 5,000 people gathered. The crowd was hungry and Jesus wanted to feed them. It was Andrew who found the boy with five small loaves of barley bread and two small fish. Jesus took the boy's lunch and fed the entire crowd.

Herod the Great

Herod the Great was the king of Judea. Romans called him "king of the Jews," but Herod was only part Jewish. Jews did not accept him as their king. Herod rebuilt many cities and even the temple, but he only pretended to worship God. He was mean to the people around him, even his own family.

Herod heard about baby Jesus who was "born King of the Jews." He was afraid Jesus would take his place as king, so he ordered all boys two years old and younger to be killed. God had other plans. An angel warned Joseph in a dream to escape to Egypt with Jesus and Mary. They stayed there until they heard that Herod had died.

JAMES AND JOHN

James and John were brothers and two of Jesus' apostles. They were fishermen until Jesus called them to be his disciples. These brothers were special to Jesus. They were with him on the mountain when Jesus' face shone like the sun and his clothes turned bright white. They were with him in the Garden of Gethsemane.

Jesus called James and John "sons of thunder." They had bad tempers. James was the first disciple killed for his faith. When Jesus was on the cross, he asked John, known as the "disciple whom Jesus loved," to care for Mary. He is the only disciple who lived to an old age.

JudaS

Judas was one of the twelve chosen by Jesus. The disciples put him in charge of keeping their money. But Judas stole money for his own use. He pretended to care about the poor, when really he was thinking about himself.

Jesus knew that Judas would betray him. While Jesus was praying in the Garden of Gethsemane, Judas brought soldiers to arrest him. They paid Judas 30 pieces of silver. After Jesus was arrested, Judas realized that he had done a terrible thing. He tried to give the money back, but it was too late. He threw the money down in the temple, and then did another terrible thing. Judas killed himself.

Mary and Martha

Mary, Martha and their brother Lazarus were friends of Jesus. He visited them at their home. Martha was very concerned with taking care of her guests. She was so busy with things, she never stopped and sat down. Mary was more relaxed. She just wanted to spend time talking with her guests, and listening to them, too.

Once, when Jesus visited their home, Martha became angry with Mary. She thought her sister should be helping her more, instead of just talking with Jesus. When she asked Jesus what he thought, he told her that it was better to spend time *with* Jesus than to be busy doing things *for* Jesus.

PONTIUS PILATE

Pontius Pilate was the Roman who allowed Jesus to be crucified. Pilate didn't understand the Jews, and the Jews didn't like him. However, when the Jews demanded that Jesus be killed, Pilate did not agree. He didn't think Jesus had done anything wrong, and he didn't believe he deserved to die. Several times, he tried to save Jesus from being crucified.

But, he was afraid that the Jews would start a riot, so he gave his permission. However, he washed his hands to show that he was not responsible for Jesus' death. In the end, he allowed Jesus to be beaten, spit on, made fun of, and finally crucified.

PaUL

Paul was one of the most important missionaries of all time. He was also an apostle, but not one of Jesus' twelve. Before he began working for God, he was called Saul. He hated Christians, and helped to persecute them. When he became a Christian, God changed his name to Paul.

Paul was called the "apostle to the Gentiles" because he preached that God was for everyone, not just Jews. He made at least three different missionary journeys where God used him to perform miracles, lead many to Christ, and encourage the Christians. Paul was beaten, thrown in prison, and killed for his belief in Jesus.

Luke

L uke was a doctor. He was also the apostle Paul's friend. He traveled with Paul during some of his missionary journeys. It is thought that Paul was sometimes sick with an unknown illness, so Luke may have been his doctor. Luke was sweet, understanding, humble, and faithful. He was also very smart, and he was a great writer.

Much of what we know about Jesus, the apostles, and Paul, is because of Luke. He wrote much about their lives and he is called an historian. His writings are in the Bible. They are the Acts of the Apostles and the Gospel of Luke. Paul was fond of his friend, and called him "beloved physician."

Other books in this series include:

The New Kids Book of Bible Passages

The New Kids Book of Bible Animals

The New Kids Book of Angel Visits